Art and Culture

Diwali

Addition and Subtraction

Joseph Otterman

Consultants

Colene Van Brunt
Math Coach
Hillsborough County Public Schools

Publishing Credits

Rachelle Cracchiolo, M.S.Ed., *Publisher*
Conni Medina, M.A.Ed., *Managing Editor*
Dona Herweck Rice, *Series Developer*
Emily R. Smith, M.A.Ed., *Series Developer*
Diana Kenney, M.A.Ed., NBCT, *Content Director*
June Kikuchi, *Content Director*
Susan Daddis, M.A.Ed., *Editor*
Stacy Monsman, M.A., *Editor*
Kevin Panter, *Senior Graphic Designer*

Image Credits: pp.4–5 Vivek Sharma/Alamy; p.10 Indiapicture/Alamy; all other images from iStock and or Shutterstock.

Library of Congress Cataloging-in-Publication Data

Names: Otterman, Joseph, 1964- author.
Title: Art and culture : Diwali / Joseph Otterman.
Description: Huntington Beach, CA : Teacher Created Materials, 2019. | Includes index. | Audience: Grades K to 3. | Description based on print version record and CIP data provided by publisher; resource not viewed.
Identifiers: LCCN 2017054960 (print) | LCCN 2018024344 (ebook) | ISBN 9781480759770 (eBook) | ISBN 9781425856830 (pbk.)
Subjects: LCSH: Divali--Juvenile literature.
Classification: LCC BL1239.82.D58 (ebook) | LCC BL1239.82.D58 O87 2019 (print) | DDC 294.5/36--dc23
LC record available at https://lccn.loc.gov/2017054960

Teacher Created Materials
5301 Oceanus Drive
Huntington Beach, CA 92649-1030
www.tcmpub.com

ISBN 978-1-4258-5683-0

Printed in China WAI002

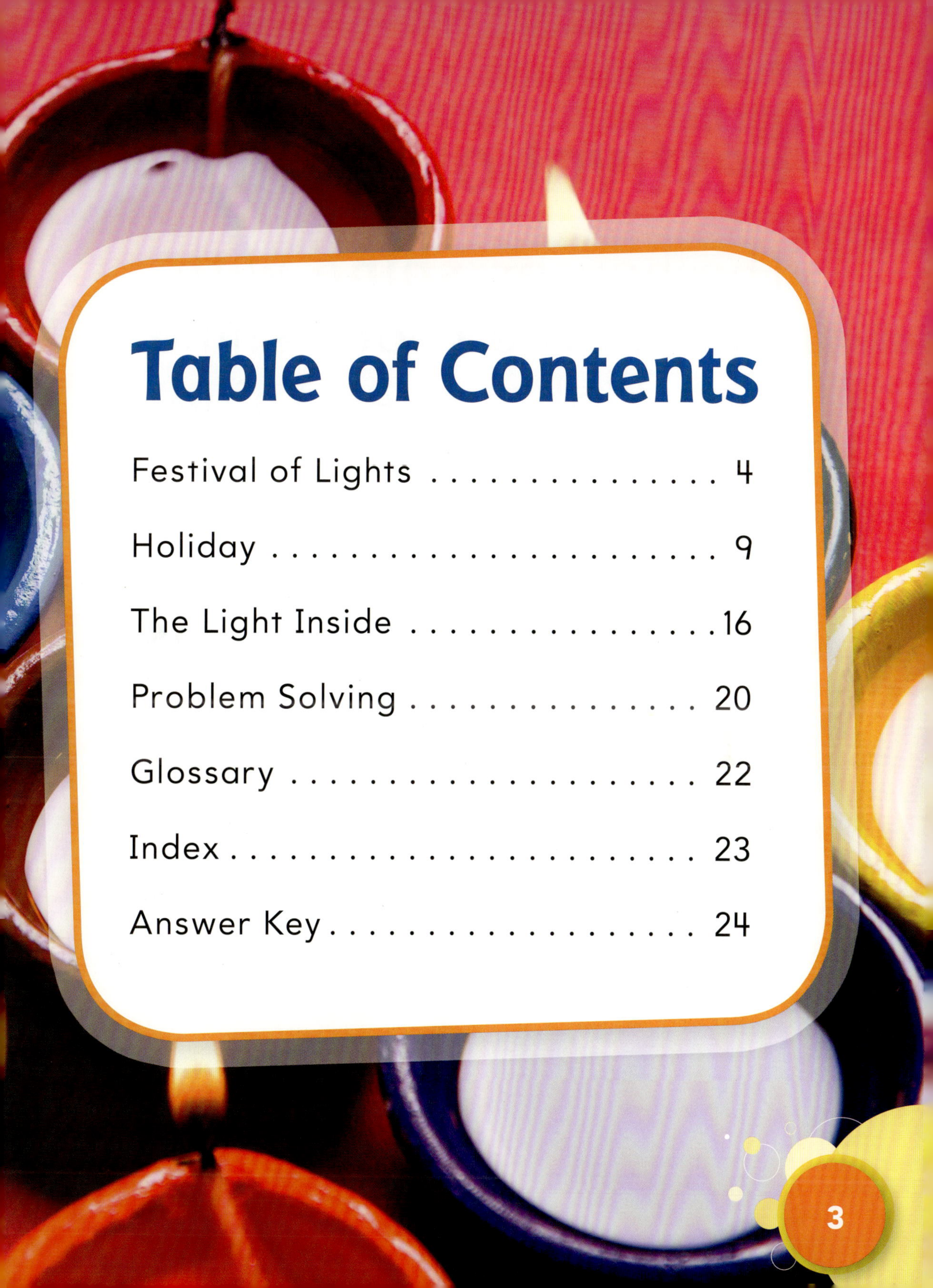

Table of Contents

Festival of Lights

The houses **shine** with lights. The roads shine, too. Lights even shine on the water! Lights are all around.

Diwali (dih-VAH-lee) is the **festival** of lights. It gets this name from lamps and candles people light.

Diwali oil lamp

Let's Do Math!

People place candles inside and outside their homes during Diwali. Imagine that there are 6 candles inside a house. There are 11 candles outside. How many more candles are outside than inside?

1. Use the picture to solve the problem.

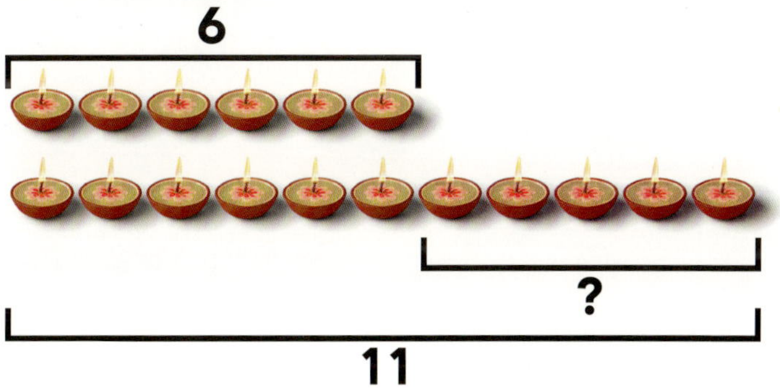

2. Which equation can help you solve the problem?

A. 6 + □ = 11

B. 6 + 11 = □

Holiday

Diwali is a **special** time. It is a holiday. It takes place mainly in India. Most people who live there take part in it.

Diwali lasts for five days. The first two days are to get ready.

People clean their homes and make them look nice. They draw pictures on the floor.

The next three days are to visit. Families gather to pray and **feast**. They laugh and share. They begin a new year. Fireworks light up the night.

Let's Do Math!

The ladoo (LAH-doo) is a treat eaten during Diwali. It is a ball-shaped dessert made with flour and sugar.

Bela has 3 almond ladoos, 4 chocolate ladoos, and 6 coconut ladoos. How many ladoos does Bela have?

1. Draw an open number line like this one. Use it to solve the problem.

2. Write an equation to show how you solved the problem.

People visit their friends, too. They wear their best clothes. They dress in bright colors. They give gifts of good luck to each other.

These friends give gifts to one another.

Let's Do Math!

Raj and Mita are giving gifts to their friends. Mita carries 4 more gifts than Raj. Raj carries 8 gifts. How many gifts does Mita carry?

1. Use the bar model to solve the problem.

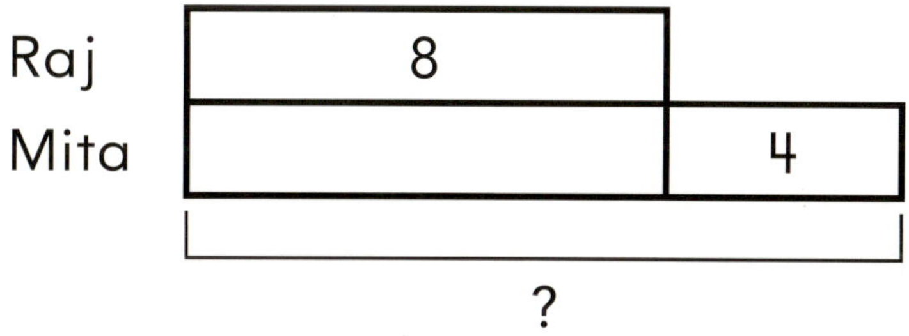

2. Choose the equations that can help you solve the problem.

A. $8 + 4 = \square$

B. $8 - 4 = \square$

C. $8 - \square = 4$

D. $4 + 8 = \square$

The Light Inside

Diwali can mean many things. But it is always about light. It is about the light in each person's heart.

The lights that are hung **remind** people of hope. They think about good things to come.

Diwali is a happy time.
It is a time to give thanks.
People give thanks for the good things in their lives.
They share that good with each other.

Problem Solving

Parties are a popular way to celebrate Diwali. Use the clues to complete the table.

1. Draw a table similar to the one on page 21.
    a. Yasin's party has 6 fewer guests than Taj's.
    b. Vari's party has 2 more guests than Yasin's.
    c. Devi's party has 4 fewer guests than Vari's.
2. Whose party has more guests: Taj's or Devi's? How many more?
3. Whose party has fewer guests: Yasin's or Devi's? How many fewer?

person having the party	number of guests
Taj	20
Yasin	
Vari	
Devi	

Glossary

feast—eat a special, big meal

festival—celebration

remind—cause someone to remember

shine—glow with light

special—different from normal

Index

Answer Key

Let's Do Math!

page 7:

1. 5 candles

2. A

page 13:

1. 13 ladoos

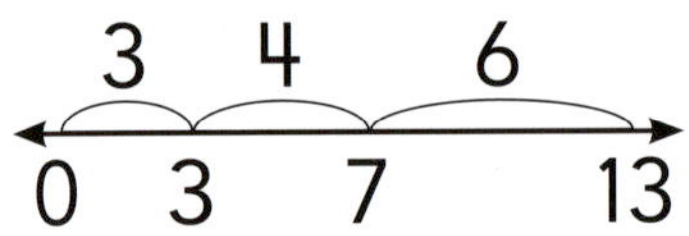

2. 3 + 4 + 6 = 13

page 15:

1. 12

2. A and D

Problem Solving

1. **a.** Yasin has 14 guests.

b. Vari has 16 guests.

c. Devi has 12 guests.

2. Taj has 8 more guests than Devi.

3. Devi has 2 fewer guests than Yasin.